50 Classic Italian Desserts

By: Kelly Johnson

Table of Contents

- Tiramisu
- Cannoli
- Panna Cotta
- Zabaglione
- Ricotta Cheesecake
- Italian Apple Cake (Torta di Mele)
- Biscotti
- Sfogliatella
- Panettone
- Cassata Siciliana
- Semifreddo
- Crostata di Frutta
- Budino (Italian Pudding)
- Ricciarelli
- Amaretti Cookies
- Bomboloni (Italian Doughnuts)
- Cantucci
- Granita
- Torta Caprese
- Gelato
- Zuccotto
- Frittelle
- Pasticciotto
- Sfogliatella Riccia
- Budino di Riso
- Sbrisolona
- Panforte
- Zeppole
- Tartufo
- Ciambella
- Sicilian Cassatelle
- Maritozzi
- Pasticceria Siciliana
- Gelo di Melone
- Crostata di Ricotta

- Semifreddo al Torrone
- Babà al Rum
- Ricotta and Chocolate Cake
- Cioccolato Fondente
- Focaccia Dolce
- Torta della Nonna
- Italian Lemon Sorbet
- Zuppa Inglese
- Vino Cotto Sorbet
- Torta di Ricotta
- Pistachio Gelato
- Panna Cotta al Caramello
- Ricotta Fritters
- Sanguinaccio Dolce
- Castel del Monte Biscuit

Tiramisu

Ingredients:

- 6 large egg yolks
- 3/4 cup granulated sugar
- 1 cup mascarpone cheese (room temperature)
- 1 1/2 cups heavy cream
- 2 cups strong brewed coffee (cooled)
- 1/4 cup coffee liqueur (optional, such as Kahlúa)
- 1 package (7 oz) ladyfingers
- 1 tablespoon unsweetened cocoa powder (for dusting)
- Dark chocolate shavings (optional, for garnish)

Instructions:

Prepare the Cream Mixture:

1. In a medium bowl, whisk the egg yolks and sugar together until smooth and pale.
2. Add the mascarpone cheese and whisk until well combined. Set this mixture aside.

Whip the Cream:

1. In a separate large bowl, beat the heavy cream with an electric mixer on medium-high speed until stiff peaks form.
2. Carefully fold the whipped cream into the mascarpone mixture, making sure to retain the airy texture.

Assemble the Tiramisu:

1. In a shallow dish, combine the brewed coffee and coffee liqueur (if using).
2. Quickly dip each ladyfinger into the coffee mixture, making sure not to soak them. Arrange a layer of dipped ladyfingers at the bottom of a 9x13-inch baking dish.

Layer the Tiramisu:

1. Spread half of the mascarpone mixture evenly over the ladyfingers.
2. Add another layer of dipped ladyfingers on top of the cream layer.
3. Top with the remaining mascarpone mixture, spreading it evenly.

Chill and Serve:

1. Cover the dish and refrigerate for at least 4 hours, preferably overnight, to allow the flavors to meld together.
2. Just before serving, dust the top with cocoa powder and garnish with chocolate shavings if desired.

Cannoli

Ingredients:

- 12 cannoli shells (store-bought or homemade)
- 2 cups ricotta cheese (drained)
- 1 cup mascarpone cheese
- 1/2 cup powdered sugar
- 1 teaspoon vanilla extract
- 1/4 cup mini chocolate chips
- Chopped pistachios (for garnish, optional)
- Powdered sugar (for dusting)

Instructions:

1. **Prepare the Filling:**
    - In a bowl, combine ricotta, mascarpone, powdered sugar, and vanilla. Stir until smooth.
    - Add mini chocolate chips and mix well.
2. **Stuff the Cannoli:**
    - Carefully pipe the filling into each cannoli shell, filling them completely.
3. **Garnish and Serve:**
    - Sprinkle with chopped pistachios and dust with powdered sugar before serving.
    - Enjoy immediately for the best crunch!

Panna Cotta

Ingredients:

- 2 cups heavy cream
- 1/2 cup whole milk
- 1/2 cup sugar
- 1 tablespoon vanilla extract
- 2 teaspoons unflavored gelatin
- 3 tablespoons water

Instructions:

1. **Prepare the Gelatin:**
    - Sprinkle gelatin over 3 tablespoons of cold water. Let it bloom for 5 minutes.
2. **Make the Panna Cotta:**
    - In a saucepan, combine heavy cream, milk, and sugar. Heat over medium until sugar dissolves, but do not bring it to a boil.
    - Remove from heat, then stir in the gelatin mixture until fully dissolved.
3. **Chill:**
    - Pour the mixture into serving cups and refrigerate for at least 4 hours, or overnight, until set.
4. **Serve:**
    - Garnish with berries, chocolate, or a drizzle of caramel before serving.

Zabaglione

Ingredients:

- 6 large egg yolks
- 1/2 cup sugar
- 1 cup Marsala wine (or sweet wine of choice)
- 1 teaspoon vanilla extract

Instructions:

1. **Prepare the Zabaglione:**
   - In a heatproof bowl, whisk egg yolks and sugar together until thickened and pale.
   - Add Marsala wine and vanilla, and continue whisking.
2. **Cook the Zabaglione:**
   - Set the bowl over a pot of simmering water (double boiler method), ensuring the bowl doesn't touch the water.
   - Whisk constantly for about 8-10 minutes, until the mixture thickens and becomes foamy.
3. **Serve:**
   - Serve warm in individual bowls or glasses, and garnish with berries or a sprinkle of cinnamon.

Ricotta Cheesecake

Ingredients:

- 2 1/2 cups ricotta cheese
- 1 cup cream cheese
- 1 1/2 cups granulated sugar
- 4 large eggs
- 1 teaspoon vanilla extract
- 1 cup sour cream
- 1/4 cup all-purpose flour
- 1/4 cup lemon zest
- 1/4 teaspoon salt

Instructions:

1. **Prepare the Crust (optional):**
   - If using a crust, prepare a graham cracker or biscuit crust and press into the bottom of a springform pan.
2. **Mix the Filling:**
   - In a bowl, combine ricotta, cream cheese, sugar, and eggs. Beat until smooth.
   - Add vanilla, sour cream, flour, lemon zest, and salt. Mix until combined.
3. **Bake:**
   - Pour the filling into the prepared crust and bake at 325°F (163°C) for 55-60 minutes, until the center is set.
4. **Chill:**
   - Let the cheesecake cool, then refrigerate for at least 4 hours before serving.

Italian Apple Cake (Torta di Mele)

Ingredients:

- 3 large apples (peeled and sliced)
- 1 1/2 cups all-purpose flour
- 1 cup sugar
- 1 teaspoon vanilla extract
- 2 teaspoons baking powder
- 1/2 teaspoon cinnamon
- 1/4 teaspoon salt
- 3 large eggs
- 1/2 cup vegetable oil
- Powdered sugar (for dusting)

Instructions:

1. **Prepare the Batter:**
   - In a large bowl, whisk together flour, sugar, baking powder, cinnamon, and salt.
   - In another bowl, beat eggs, oil, and vanilla. Add the dry ingredients and mix well.
2. **Combine Apples:**
   - Gently fold the apple slices into the batter, then pour the mixture into a greased baking pan.
3. **Bake:**
   - Bake at 350°F (175°C) for 40-45 minutes or until a toothpick comes out clean.
4. **Serve:**
   - Dust with powdered sugar and enjoy!

Biscotti

Ingredients:

- 2 cups all-purpose flour
- 1 cup sugar
- 1 teaspoon baking powder
- 1/2 teaspoon salt
- 3 large eggs
- 1 teaspoon vanilla extract
- 1/2 cup almonds (or other nuts)
- 1/2 teaspoon almond extract (optional)

Instructions:

1. **Prepare the Dough:**
   - In a bowl, combine flour, sugar, baking powder, and salt. Add eggs and vanilla, and mix until dough forms.
   - Fold in almonds (and almond extract if using).
2. **Shape and Bake:**
   - Shape the dough into a log on a baking sheet and bake at 350°F (175°C) for 25-30 minutes.
   - Remove from the oven, slice diagonally, and bake again for 10-12 minutes to crisp.

Sfogliatella

Ingredients:

- 1 package puff pastry
- 2 cups ricotta cheese
- 1/2 cup semolina flour
- 1/2 cup sugar
- 1 tablespoon orange zest
- 1 teaspoon vanilla extract
- Powdered sugar (for dusting)

Instructions:

1. **Prepare the Filling:**
   - In a saucepan, cook semolina, sugar, and ricotta until thickened. Remove from heat and stir in orange zest and vanilla.
2. **Shape the Pastries:**
   - Roll out puff pastry and cut into circles. Place a spoonful of filling in the center and fold the edges to form a shell shape.
3. **Bake:**
   - Bake at 375°F (190°C) for 20-25 minutes until golden brown.
4. **Serve:**
   - Dust with powdered sugar before serving.

Panettone

Ingredients:

- 4 cups all-purpose flour
- 1/2 cup sugar
- 1 teaspoon salt
- 2 teaspoons active dry yeast
- 1/2 cup milk
- 1/4 cup water
- 4 large eggs
- 1/2 cup butter (softened)
- 1 cup mixed dried fruit (raisins, currants)
- 1/2 cup candied orange peel

Instructions:

1. **Prepare the Dough:**
   - Mix flour, sugar, salt, and yeast. Add milk, water, eggs, and butter. Knead until smooth.
2. **Let it Rise:**
   - Allow the dough to rise for 2 hours. Add dried fruit and orange peel, then shape into a loaf.
3. **Bake:**
   - Bake at 350°F (175°C) for 40-45 minutes until golden.

Cassata Siciliana

Ingredients:

- 1 sponge cake
- 1 cup ricotta cheese
- 1/4 cup sugar
- 1/4 teaspoon vanilla extract
- 1/4 cup candied fruit (for garnish)
- Marzipan (for coating)

Instructions:

1. **Prepare the Filling:**
    - Mix ricotta, sugar, and vanilla together until smooth.
2. **Assemble:**
    - Slice the sponge cake and layer with ricotta filling. Cover with marzipan and garnish with candied fruit.

Semifreddo

Ingredients:

- 2 cups heavy cream
- 1 cup sugar
- 4 large egg yolks
- 1 teaspoon vanilla extract

Instructions:

1. **Whisk the Egg Yolks:**
    - Beat egg yolks and sugar together until thickened.
2. **Whip the Cream:**
    - Whip heavy cream to stiff peaks and fold into egg mixture.
3. **Freeze:**
    - Pour into molds and freeze for at least 4 hours.

Crostata di Frutta

Ingredients:

- 1 package shortcrust pastry
- 2 cups pastry cream
- Fresh fruit (berries, kiwi, etc.)

Instructions:

1. **Prepare the Crust:**
    - Roll out the pastry and bake according to package instructions.
2. **Fill the Tart:**
    - Fill the baked crust with pastry cream and arrange fresh fruit on top.

Budino (Italian Pudding)

Ingredients:

- 2 cups whole milk
- 1/2 cup sugar
- 2 tablespoons cornstarch
- 1 teaspoon vanilla extract

Instructions:

1. **Cook the Pudding:**
    - Combine milk, sugar, and cornstarch in a saucepan. Cook over medium heat, whisking constantly, until thickened.
2. **Chill and Serve:**
    - Let cool, then refrigerate for at least 2 hours before serving.

Ricciarelli

Ingredients:

- 2 cups almond flour
- 1 cup powdered sugar
- 2 large egg whites
- 1 teaspoon almond extract

Instructions:

1. **Prepare the Dough:**
   - Mix almond flour, powdered sugar, egg whites, and almond extract into a dough.
2. **Shape and Bake:**
   - Shape into small oval cookies and bake at 325°F (165°C) for 10-12 minutes.

Amaretti Cookies

Ingredients:

- 2 cups almond flour
- 1 cup powdered sugar
- 2 large egg whites
- 1 teaspoon almond extract
- 1/2 teaspoon vanilla extract
- Pinch of salt
- Extra sugar for rolling

Instructions:

1. **Prepare the Dough:**
   - Mix almond flour, powdered sugar, and salt in a bowl. Add egg whites, almond extract, and vanilla. Stir until combined into a sticky dough.
2. **Shape the Cookies:**
   - Roll the dough into small balls, then roll in sugar.
3. **Bake:**
   - Place the cookies on a baking sheet and bake at 325°F (165°C) for 15-18 minutes until lightly golden.
4. **Cool:**
   - Let cool on a wire rack before serving.

Bomboloni (Italian Doughnuts)

Ingredients:

- 4 cups all-purpose flour
- 1/2 cup sugar
- 2 teaspoons active dry yeast
- 1 cup warm milk
- 4 tablespoons unsalted butter (melted)
- 2 large eggs
- 1/2 teaspoon salt
- Vegetable oil for frying
- Powdered sugar for dusting
- Jam or custard for filling

Instructions:

1. **Make the Dough:**
   - In a bowl, mix yeast with warm milk and a pinch of sugar. Let sit for 5 minutes.
   - Add flour, sugar, melted butter, eggs, and salt. Knead until smooth and elastic. Let rise for 1-2 hours.
2. **Shape the Bomboloni:**
   - Roll the dough out and cut into circles. Let rise for another 30 minutes.
3. **Fry:**
   - Heat oil to 350°F (175°C) and fry the doughnuts until golden on each side.
4. **Fill and Serve:**
   - Fill with jam or custard, dust with powdered sugar, and serve warm.

Cantucci

Ingredients:

- 2 cups all-purpose flour
- 1 cup sugar
- 1/2 teaspoon baking powder
- 1/4 teaspoon salt
- 2 large eggs
- 1/2 cup almonds (toasted and chopped)
- 1 teaspoon vanilla extract

Instructions:

1. **Make the Dough:**
   - Mix flour, sugar, baking powder, and salt in a bowl. Add eggs and vanilla, and stir until a dough forms. Fold in the almonds.
2. **Shape the Dough:**
   - Shape the dough into two logs and place them on a baking sheet. Bake at 350°F (175°C) for 20 minutes.
3. **Slice and Bake Again:**
   - Slice the logs into diagonal pieces and bake for another 10 minutes to crisp.

Granita

Ingredients:

- 2 cups water
- 1 cup sugar
- 1 1/2 cups fruit puree (such as lemon, strawberry, or coffee)
- 1 teaspoon lemon juice

Instructions:

1. **Make the Syrup:**
    - In a saucepan, combine water and sugar. Heat until the sugar dissolves, then let cool.
2. **Combine with Fruit:**
    - Mix the syrup with fruit puree and lemon juice.
3. **Freeze:**
    - Pour the mixture into a shallow pan and freeze. Stir every 30 minutes with a fork to create a slushy texture.

Torta Caprese

Ingredients:

- 2 cups almond flour
- 1 cup dark chocolate (melted)
- 1/2 cup butter (melted)
- 3/4 cup sugar
- 4 large eggs
- 1/4 teaspoon salt
- Powdered sugar for dusting

Instructions:

1. **Prepare the Batter:**
    - Beat the eggs and sugar until light and fluffy. Add melted chocolate, butter, almond flour, and salt. Stir until smooth.
2. **Bake:**
    - Pour the batter into a greased pan and bake at 350°F (175°C) for 30-35 minutes.
3. **Serve:**
    - Let cool, then dust with powdered sugar and serve.

Gelato

Ingredients:

- 2 cups whole milk
- 1 cup heavy cream
- 3/4 cup sugar
- 4 large egg yolks
- 1 teaspoon vanilla extract

Instructions:

1. **Make the Base:**
    - In a saucepan, heat milk and cream until warm. In a bowl, whisk egg yolks with sugar, then add the warm milk mixture slowly.
2. **Cook the Mixture:**
    - Return to the saucepan and cook over low heat, stirring constantly, until it thickens.
3. **Cool and Freeze:**
    - Let the mixture cool, then add vanilla extract. Pour into an ice cream maker and churn according to instructions.

Zuccotto

Ingredients:

- 1 sponge cake (store-bought or homemade)
- 1 cup ricotta cheese
- 1/2 cup mascarpone cheese
- 1/2 cup sugar
- 1/4 cup dark chocolate (melted)
- 1 tablespoon rum (optional)
- Cocoa powder for dusting

Instructions:

1. **Prepare the Filling:**
    - Mix ricotta, mascarpone, sugar, and melted chocolate until smooth. Add rum if desired.
2. **Assemble the Zuccotto:**
    - Line a bowl with slices of sponge cake, then fill with the ricotta mixture. Cover with more cake and chill for at least 4 hours.
3. **Serve:**
    - Unmold and dust with cocoa powder before serving.

Frittelle

Ingredients:

- 2 cups all-purpose flour
- 1 tablespoon sugar
- 2 teaspoons active dry yeast
- 1/2 teaspoon salt
- 3/4 cup warm water
- 1/2 teaspoon vanilla extract
- Vegetable oil for frying
- Powdered sugar for dusting

Instructions:

1. **Prepare the Dough:**
     - Mix flour, sugar, yeast, and salt. Add warm water and vanilla and knead until smooth. Let rise for 1 hour.
2. **Fry:**
     - Heat oil to 350°F (175°C) and fry spoonfuls of dough until golden.
3. **Serve:**
     - Dust with powdered sugar and serve warm.

Pasticciotto

Ingredients:

- 2 cups all-purpose flour
- 1/2 cup sugar
- 1/2 cup butter
- 1 large egg
- 1/2 teaspoon vanilla extract
- 1 cup pastry cream (for filling)

Instructions:

1. **Make the Dough:**
    - Mix flour, sugar, butter, egg, and vanilla to form a dough. Chill for 30 minutes.
2. **Fill and Bake:**
    - Roll out dough and cut into circles. Place pastry cream in the center and seal. Bake at 350°F (175°C) for 20-25 minutes.

Sfogliatella Riccia

Ingredients:

- 2 cups ricotta cheese
- 1 cup semolina flour
- 1/4 cup sugar
- 1 teaspoon vanilla extract
- 1 package puff pastry
- Powdered sugar for dusting

Instructions:

1. **Make the Filling:**
    - Cook semolina and sugar in a saucepan with ricotta until thick. Stir in vanilla extract.
2. **Shape the Pastries:**
    - Roll out puff pastry and cut into circles. Place filling in the center and fold into a shell shape.
3. **Bake:**
    - Bake at 375°F (190°C) for 25-30 minutes until golden brown. Dust with powdered sugar before serving.

Budino di Riso

Ingredients:

- 1 cup Arborio rice
- 4 cups whole milk
- 1/2 cup sugar
- 1 teaspoon vanilla extract
- 1 tablespoon lemon zest
- 2 eggs, beaten
- 1/2 cup raisins (optional)
- 1 tablespoon butter

Instructions:

1. **Cook the Rice:**
    - In a saucepan, cook rice in 2 cups of milk over medium heat until soft, about 15-20 minutes.
2. **Make the Pudding:**
    - Add the remaining milk, sugar, and vanilla to the rice mixture. Stir constantly until it thickens, about 10 minutes.
3. **Finish the Pudding:**
    - Remove from heat and stir in beaten eggs, lemon zest, and raisins. Pour into a greased mold.
4. **Chill:**
    - Let the pudding cool, then refrigerate for at least 4 hours. Serve chilled with a dusting of cinnamon.

Sbrisolona

Ingredients:

- 2 cups all-purpose flour
- 1 cup cornmeal
- 1 cup sugar
- 1/2 cup butter (cold and cubed)
- 1/4 cup slivered almonds
- 1/2 teaspoon vanilla extract
- 1 egg

Instructions:

1. **Make the Dough:**
    - Mix flour, cornmeal, sugar, and almonds in a bowl. Add cold butter and mix with your hands until the mixture resembles breadcrumbs.
2. **Add Wet Ingredients:**
    - Beat the egg with vanilla and stir it into the dough. Form a dough but keep it crumbly.
3. **Bake:**
    - Press the dough into a round pan and bake at 350°F (175°C) for 30-40 minutes until golden.

Panforte

Ingredients:

- 1 cup almonds, toasted
- 1 cup hazelnuts, toasted
- 1 cup dried figs, chopped
- 1/2 cup sugar
- 1/4 cup honey
- 1 tablespoon cocoa powder
- 1 teaspoon cinnamon
- 1/2 teaspoon nutmeg
- 1/4 teaspoon ground cloves
- 2 tablespoons flour

Instructions:

1. **Prepare the Nuts:**
    - Toast the almonds and hazelnuts in a dry pan. Chop the figs.
2. **Make the Syrup:**
    - Heat sugar and honey in a saucepan until dissolved, then add cocoa powder and spices.
3. **Mix the Ingredients:**
    - Combine the nuts, figs, and flour in a bowl. Pour the syrup over and mix well.
4. **Bake:**
    - Press the mixture into a round pan and bake at 325°F (160°C) for 30 minutes. Let cool before slicing.

Zeppole

Ingredients:

- 1 cup water
- 1/2 cup butter
- 1 cup all-purpose flour
- 4 large eggs
- 1/4 teaspoon salt
- Vegetable oil for frying
- Powdered sugar for dusting
- Ricotta cheese or pastry cream for filling

Instructions:

1. **Make the Dough:**
    - Bring water and butter to a boil, then stir in flour and salt. Cook for 2 minutes, then remove from heat and mix in eggs one at a time.
2. **Fry the Zeppole:**
    - Heat oil to 350°F (175°C) and drop spoonfuls of dough into the oil. Fry until golden and drain on paper towels.
3. **Fill and Serve:**
    - Fill with ricotta cheese or pastry cream. Dust with powdered sugar before serving.

Tartufo

Ingredients:

- 2 cups vanilla ice cream
- 1 cup chocolate ice cream
- 1/2 cup crushed hazelnuts
- 1/4 cup dark chocolate (melted)
- Cocoa powder for dusting

Instructions:

1. **Form the Ice Cream Balls:**
   - Scoop a small ball of vanilla ice cream and form it into a sphere. Scoop chocolate ice cream and insert it into the center of the vanilla ball. Freeze.
2. **Coat the Tartufo:**
   - Roll the frozen ice cream in crushed hazelnuts and melted chocolate.
3. **Serve:**
   - Dust with cocoa powder and serve immediately.

Ciambella

Ingredients:

- 2 cups all-purpose flour
- 1 cup sugar
- 4 large eggs
- 1/2 cup vegetable oil
- 1 teaspoon vanilla extract
- 1 tablespoon baking powder
- 1/2 teaspoon salt
- Powdered sugar for dusting

Instructions:

1. **Make the Batter:**
   - Mix flour, sugar, salt, and baking powder in a bowl. Beat eggs, oil, and vanilla in a separate bowl. Combine both mixtures.
2. **Bake:**
   - Pour the batter into a ring mold and bake at 350°F (175°C) for 40-45 minutes.
3. **Serve:**
   - Let the cake cool and dust with powdered sugar before serving.

Sicilian Cassatelle

Ingredients:

- 2 cups ricotta cheese
- 1/2 cup powdered sugar
- 1 teaspoon vanilla extract
- 1/4 teaspoon cinnamon
- 1 package puff pastry
- Vegetable oil for frying

Instructions:

1. **Make the Filling:**
    - Mix ricotta, powdered sugar, vanilla, and cinnamon until smooth.
2. **Shape the Cassatelle:**
    - Roll out puff pastry and cut into circles. Place a spoonful of filling in the center and fold to seal.
3. **Fry:**
    - Heat oil to 350°F (175°C) and fry the cassatelle until golden.
4. **Serve:**
    - Drain on paper towels and serve warm.

Maritozzi

Ingredients:

- 2 cups all-purpose flour
- 1/2 cup sugar
- 1/4 cup milk
- 1/4 cup butter (melted)
- 2 teaspoons active dry yeast
- 1/2 teaspoon salt
- 2 large eggs
- 1 teaspoon vanilla extract
- Whipped cream for filling

Instructions:

1. **Make the Dough:**
    - Mix warm milk, yeast, sugar, and salt. Add flour, eggs, melted butter, and vanilla. Knead until smooth. Let rise for 1 hour.
2. **Shape the Dough:**
    - Divide dough into small portions and shape into buns. Let rise for 30 minutes.
3. **Bake:**
    - Bake at 350°F (175°C) for 15-20 minutes until golden. Let cool.
4. **Fill and Serve:**
    - Slice and fill with whipped cream before serving.

Pasticceria Siciliana

Ingredients:

- 2 cups ricotta cheese
- 1/2 cup powdered sugar
- 1 teaspoon vanilla extract
- 1 cup almond flour
- 1/4 cup chocolate chips
- 1 tablespoon honey
- 1/2 teaspoon cinnamon

Instructions:

1. **Prepare the Filling:**
    - Mix ricotta, powdered sugar, vanilla, honey, cinnamon, and almond flour until smooth.
2. **Shape the Pastries:**
    - Fill small pastry shells with the ricotta mixture and top with chocolate chips.
3. **Serve:**
    - Serve the pastries chilled or at room temperature.

Gelo di Melone

Ingredients:

- 4 cups watermelon juice (strained)
- 1/2 cup sugar
- 1 tablespoon lemon juice
- 1 tablespoon cornstarch
- Chopped pistachios (optional)
- Chocolate chips (optional)

Instructions:

1. **Prepare the Mixture:**
    - In a saucepan, combine watermelon juice, sugar, and lemon juice. Heat over medium until it starts to simmer.
2. **Thicken the Mixture:**
    - In a small bowl, dissolve cornstarch in 1/4 cup of water. Slowly add it to the watermelon mixture, stirring constantly until it thickens.
3. **Chill:**
    - Pour the mixture into molds and refrigerate for at least 3 hours until set.
4. **Serve:**
    - Unmold the gelo di melone and garnish with pistachios or chocolate chips before serving.

Crostata di Ricotta

Ingredients:

- 1 1/2 cups all-purpose flour
- 1/2 cup sugar
- 1/2 cup unsalted butter (cold)
- 1 egg
- 1/2 teaspoon vanilla extract
- 1/2 teaspoon baking powder
- 1 1/2 cups ricotta cheese
- 1/4 cup powdered sugar
- Zest of 1 lemon

Instructions:

1. **Make the Dough:**
   - Mix flour, sugar, and baking powder in a bowl. Add cold butter and rub together to form a crumbly mixture. Add the egg and vanilla, then knead into a dough.
2. **Prepare the Filling:**
   - In a separate bowl, mix ricotta, powdered sugar, and lemon zest until smooth.
3. **Assemble the Tart:**
   - Roll out the dough and press it into a tart pan. Spread the ricotta filling evenly over the base.
4. **Bake:**
   - Bake at 350°F (175°C) for 30-35 minutes until golden. Let cool before serving.

Semifreddo al Torrone

Ingredients:

- 2 cups heavy cream
- 1 cup milk
- 3/4 cup sugar
- 1/2 cup torrone (Italian nougat), chopped
- 1/4 teaspoon vanilla extract
- 2 egg yolks

Instructions:

1. **Prepare the Custard:**
   - In a saucepan, heat milk and sugar until warm. In a separate bowl, whisk egg yolks, then slowly pour in the warm milk mixture, whisking constantly. Cook until thickened.
2. **Chill the Custard:**
   - Remove from heat and let cool. Add vanilla extract and refrigerate until fully chilled.
3. **Whip the Cream:**
   - Whip the heavy cream to stiff peaks, then fold it into the chilled custard.
4. **Assemble the Semifreddo:**
   - Gently fold in chopped torrone and pour the mixture into a loaf pan. Freeze for 6 hours or overnight.
5. **Serve:**
   - Slice and serve directly from the freezer.

Babà al Rum

Ingredients:

- 1 1/2 cups all-purpose flour
- 1/2 cup sugar
- 1/2 cup unsalted butter (melted)
- 3 large eggs
- 1/2 cup warm milk
- 2 teaspoons dry yeast
- 1/4 cup rum
- 1/2 cup water
- 1 cup sugar (for syrup)

Instructions:

1. **Prepare the Dough:**
    - Dissolve yeast in warm milk and sugar. Let it sit for 10 minutes. Mix in flour, melted butter, and eggs. Knead the dough until smooth.
2. **Let the Dough Rise:**
    - Cover and let the dough rise in a warm place for 1 hour.
3. **Bake:**
    - Divide the dough into small molds and bake at 350°F (175°C) for 20-25 minutes until golden.
4. **Prepare the Syrup:**
    - In a saucepan, combine water and sugar. Boil for 5 minutes, then add rum.
5. **Soak the Babà:**
    - Once the babà cakes have cooled, soak them in the rum syrup. Serve immediately.

Ricotta and Chocolate Cake

Ingredients:

- 2 cups ricotta cheese
- 1 1/2 cups sugar
- 2 cups all-purpose flour
- 1/2 cup unsweetened cocoa powder
- 1 teaspoon baking powder
- 1/2 teaspoon vanilla extract
- 2 large eggs
- 1/2 cup melted butter

Instructions:

1. **Make the Batter:**
    - Beat the ricotta cheese, sugar, eggs, and vanilla until smooth. Add flour, cocoa powder, and baking powder. Mix in the melted butter.
2. **Bake:**
    - Pour the batter into a greased cake pan and bake at 350°F (175°C) for 30-35 minutes.
3. **Serve:**
    - Let the cake cool before slicing and serving.

Cioccolato Fondente

Ingredients:

- 8 oz dark chocolate (70% cocoa)
- 1/2 cup heavy cream
- 2 tablespoons unsalted butter
- 1 tablespoon sugar (optional)

Instructions:

1. **Melt the Chocolate:**
   - In a heatproof bowl, melt the chocolate over a double boiler or microwave.
2. **Add Cream and Butter:**
   - Stir in heavy cream and butter until smooth. Add sugar if desired.
3. **Serve:**
   - Dip fruits or pastries into the melted chocolate or drizzle over desserts.

Focaccia Dolce

Ingredients:

- 2 cups all-purpose flour
- 1 cup warm milk
- 1 tablespoon sugar
- 2 teaspoons active dry yeast
- 1/4 cup olive oil
- 1/2 teaspoon salt
- 1/4 cup honey
- Powdered sugar for dusting

Instructions:

1. **Prepare the Dough:**
    - Mix warm milk, sugar, and yeast in a bowl. Let it sit for 5 minutes to activate. Add flour, olive oil, and salt to form a dough. Knead until smooth.
2. **Let the Dough Rise:**
    - Cover and let rise for 1 hour.
3. **Bake:**
    - Shape the dough into a rectangular form and bake at 350°F (175°C) for 20 minutes until golden.
4. **Serve:**
    - Drizzle with honey and dust with powdered sugar before serving.

Torta della Nonna

Ingredients:

- 1 sheet puff pastry
- 2 cups ricotta cheese
- 1/2 cup powdered sugar
- 1/2 teaspoon vanilla extract
- 1 egg
- Pine nuts for garnish

Instructions:

1. **Prepare the Filling:**
    - Mix ricotta, powdered sugar, vanilla extract, and egg until smooth.
2. **Assemble the Cake:**
    - Place puff pastry in a tart pan, fill with the ricotta mixture, and top with pine nuts.
3. **Bake:**
    - Bake at 350°F (175°C) for 30-35 minutes until golden.
4. **Serve:**
    - Let cool before serving.

Italian Lemon Sorbet

Ingredients:

- 1 1/2 cups fresh lemon juice
- 1 cup sugar
- 2 cups water
- Zest of 1 lemon

Instructions:

1. **Make the Syrup:**
     - Combine water and sugar in a saucepan. Heat until the sugar dissolves. Let cool.
2. **Combine Ingredients:**
     - Mix the syrup with lemon juice and zest. Pour into an ice cream maker and churn until thickened.
3. **Freeze and Serve:**
     - Freeze the sorbet for at least 4 hours before serving.

Zuppa Inglese

Ingredients:

- 2 cups custard (prepared)
- 1 cup chocolate pudding (prepared)
- 2 cups strong coffee (cooled)
- 1/4 cup rum (optional)
- 1 package sponge cake or ladyfingers
- 1/2 cup cocoa powder (for dusting)

Instructions:

1. **Prepare the Layers:**
    - Slice the sponge cake or ladyfingers and soak each piece in the coffee and rum mixture.
2. **Assemble the Zuppa:**
    - Layer the soaked cake in a trifle dish or serving glasses, alternating between custard and chocolate pudding layers.
3. **Chill:**
    - Refrigerate for at least 4 hours, allowing the flavors to meld together.
4. **Serve:**
    - Dust with cocoa powder before serving.

Vino Cotto Sorbet

Ingredients:

- 2 cups vino cotto (Italian cooked wine syrup)
- 1/2 cup sugar
- 1 cup water
- 1 tablespoon lemon juice

Instructions:

1. **Prepare the Syrup:**
    - In a saucepan, combine sugar and water, heating until sugar dissolves. Add vino cotto and lemon juice, and let it simmer for a few minutes.
2. **Chill:**
    - Allow the syrup to cool completely before placing it in an ice cream maker.
3. **Churn:**
    - Churn in an ice cream maker according to the manufacturer's instructions until it reaches sorbet consistency.
4. **Serve:**
    - Transfer to a container and freeze for at least 2 hours before serving.

Torta di Ricotta

Ingredients:

- 1 1/2 cups ricotta cheese
- 1 1/2 cups sugar
- 1 1/2 cups all-purpose flour
- 1/2 cup butter (softened)
- 3 large eggs
- 1 teaspoon vanilla extract
- Zest of 1 lemon
- 1/2 teaspoon baking powder

Instructions:

1. **Make the Batter:**
    - In a large bowl, beat together ricotta, sugar, butter, eggs, and vanilla. Add the flour, baking powder, and lemon zest, mixing until smooth.
2. **Bake:**
    - Pour the batter into a greased cake pan and bake at 350°F (175°C) for 40-45 minutes, until a toothpick inserted comes out clean.
3. **Serve:**
    - Let cool before slicing and serving.

Pistachio Gelato

Ingredients:

- 1 cup shelled pistachios
- 2 cups whole milk
- 1 cup heavy cream
- 1/2 cup sugar
- 4 large egg yolks
- 1/2 teaspoon vanilla extract

Instructions:

1. **Blend the Pistachios:**
    - Blend pistachios with a small amount of milk until smooth, forming a pistachio paste.
2. **Prepare the Custard:**
    - In a saucepan, heat the milk and cream. In a separate bowl, whisk egg yolks and sugar. Gradually combine with the warm milk mixture, cooking until thickened.
3. **Churn the Gelato:**
    - Stir in the pistachio paste and vanilla, then chill the mixture in the refrigerator for a few hours. Churn in an ice cream maker until thickened.
4. **Freeze and Serve:**
    - Freeze for a few more hours before serving.

Panna Cotta al Caramello

Ingredients:

- 2 cups heavy cream
- 1 cup whole milk
- 1/2 cup sugar
- 1 tablespoon gelatin
- 1/4 cup water
- 1/2 teaspoon vanilla extract
- 1/2 cup caramel sauce (store-bought or homemade)

Instructions:

1. **Prepare the Gelatin:**
    - Dissolve the gelatin in water and let it bloom for 5 minutes.
2. **Cook the Cream Mixture:**
    - Heat heavy cream, milk, and sugar in a saucepan over medium heat. Once the sugar dissolves, remove from heat and stir in the gelatin.
3. **Assemble the Panna Cotta:**
    - Pour the cream mixture into individual cups and refrigerate for at least 4 hours to set.
4. **Top with Caramel:**
    - Before serving, top with caramel sauce.

Ricotta Fritters

Ingredients:

- 1 1/2 cups ricotta cheese
- 1/2 cup flour
- 1/4 cup sugar
- 1/2 teaspoon baking powder
- 1/4 teaspoon cinnamon (optional)
- Vegetable oil (for frying)
- Powdered sugar (for dusting)

Instructions:

1. **Make the Batter:**
    - Mix ricotta, flour, sugar, baking powder, and cinnamon until combined.
2. **Fry the Fritters:**
    - Heat oil in a pan over medium heat. Drop spoonfuls of the batter into the hot oil and fry until golden brown, about 2-3 minutes per side.
3. **Serve:**
    - Drain on paper towels, dust with powdered sugar, and serve warm.

Sanguinaccio Dolce

Ingredients:

- 2 cups whole milk
- 1/2 cup sugar
- 1/4 cup unsweetened cocoa powder
- 2 ounces dark chocolate (chopped)
- 3 tablespoons cornstarch
- 1/2 cup red wine (optional)
- 1/2 teaspoon vanilla extract

Instructions:

1. **Prepare the Mixture:**
   - In a saucepan, combine milk, sugar, cocoa powder, and cornstarch. Whisk until smooth.
2. **Cook the Custard:**
   - Heat the mixture over medium heat, whisking constantly, until it thickens. Add the chocolate, wine, and vanilla, stirring until the chocolate melts.
3. **Serve:**
   - Allow the pudding to cool before serving. Serve with cookies or fruit.

Castel del Monte Biscuit

Ingredients:

- 2 cups all-purpose flour
- 1/2 cup sugar
- 1/4 teaspoon cinnamon
- 1/4 teaspoon nutmeg
- 1/2 teaspoon baking powder
- 1/2 cup unsalted butter (softened)
- 1 large egg
- 1 teaspoon vanilla extract
- Zest of 1 lemon

Instructions:

1. **Prepare the Dough:**
    - Mix flour, sugar, cinnamon, nutmeg, and baking powder. Add softened butter, egg, vanilla, and lemon zest, mixing until a dough forms.
2. **Shape the Biscuits:**
    - Roll out the dough and cut into desired shapes.
3. **Bake:**
    - Bake at 350°F (175°C) for 15-20 minutes until golden.
4. **Serve:**
    - Let cool before serving.